The Laurel Canyon Vegetarian Cookbook
is dedicated to the original cook in my life,
my mother, Regina Sammon Weigel (1923–1984),
who taught me how to cook and so much more,
and to all mothers and cooks everywhere.
I also dedicate this cookbook to my husband, Ken Sargent.
Without his beautiful photography,
patience, kindness, and love, this book would not exist.

The Laurel Canyon Vegetarian Cookbook

California Cosmic Consciousness Cooking

Sonya Maria Sargent
Photographs by Ken Sargent

RAYMOND
·PRESS·

Published by Raymond Press
An imprint of Prospect Park Books
2359 Lincoln Avenue
Altadena, California 91001
www.prospectparkbooks.com

Library of Congress of Cataloging in Publication data is on file with the Library of Congress.
The following is for reference only:
The Laurel Canyon Vegetarian Cookbook: California Cosmic Consciousness Cooking
Subjects: 1. Cooking, vegetarian. 2. Cooking, California.
ISBN: 978-1-945551-83-3

Photography by Ken Sargent

Design by Amy Inouye, Future Studio
Layout by Julianne Johnson

Printed in the United States of America

Contents

Introduction

What is Laurel Canyon and where is it? Laurel Canyon, discovered in 1910, is a paradise of contradictions. It is a small group of winding roads that looks like the country, nestled right in the hills above the big, old city of Los Angeles. It's woodsy, forest-like, and in harmony with nature while being ten minutes away from the world-famous Whisky-a-Go-Go on the Sunset Strip, right in the center of Hollywood, California.

It is one of the canyon roads that connects Los Angeles with the San Fernando Valley. The street, Laurel Canyon Boulevard, stretches from Crescent Heights and Sunset Boulevard in West Hollywood all the way to the San Fernando Mission in Mission Hills. Originally, in 1907, it was an 82-mile dirt road that ran up the canyon, dividing at what is now called Lookout Mountain Road. One road went up to the top of Lookout Mountain; the other, to the top of the Santa Monica Mountains and then down into the San Fernando Valley.

What is the Laurel Canyon vibe? Laid-back, for sure. Casual, come-as-you-are, kick-back, natural, quiet, and peaceful—most of the time. Except when talented musicians are cranking up their guitars, keyboards, or drums. Artists, celebrities, and stars of all kinds once ruled Laurel Canyon. From magician/escape artist Harry Houdini in the 1920s to Governor Jerry Brown in the 1970s to musical greats like the Byrds, Jackson Browne, the Monkees, Love, Crosby, Stills & Nash, the Mamas and the Papas, Joni Mitchell, Carole King, the Eagles, and Jim Morrison of the Doors, many legendary people lived here and made their music here. Currently, alt-rock "Summertime Sadness" singer Lana Del Rey is renting a home in Laurel Canyon.

The eclectic house styles of Laurel Canyon include Spanish hacienda, log cabin, English Tudor, Cape Cod, bungalow, A-frame mountain retreat/chalet, and Mediterranean mansion. One style nestles next to another, peacefully creating a very colorful neighborhood. Laurel Canyon has few commercial businesses: the cozy Canyon Country Store Market, the Bohemian Pace Restaurant, and the Laurel Canyon Dry Cleaners. Everything you need!

So, what does all this have to do with a vegetarian cookbook? In the many years I have lived here, I have learned to cook vegetarian, vegan, and non-vegetarian. And I'm still learning and trying out new recipes! I have hosted or been a guest at many dinner parties, Thanksgiving dinners, picnics, and potluck meals with Canyon neighbors, family, and friends. I wrote *The Laurel Canyon Vegetarian Cookbook* to share these recipes with you and to bring a taste of the Laurel Canyon sunshine and positive vibe into your kitchen and around your dinner table.

Even if you are not a vegetarian or vegan, there are bound to be family members and friends of yours that have gone vegetarian. Whatever their reasons, you will be able to impress your dinner guests with marvelous vegetarian meals. The recipes in this cookbook are natural, easy, fast, and cheap. I use ingredients that you probably have on hand in your kitchen already. The best things in life are cheap, if not free. You don't have to spend a lot of money to eat well. The directions in my recipes cut to the chase and are easy to follow for people who don't have time to spend hours cooking. So, lighten up. Become enlightened...*The Laurel Canyon Vegetarian Cookbook* way!

Vegetarian Protein

We all need protein to give us energy and make our hair shine. According to the Vegetarian Resource Group, a vegan source, the protein recommendation for a 154-pound male per day is **56-70** grams. For a 126-pound female, it is **46-58** grams. The recommended daily allowance is about 0.36 grams of protein per each pound we weigh.

I have made a chart with the protein grams for some of the foods in this cookbook. With a little math, you should be able to get your daily protein portion. For a more detailed protein and nutritional breakdown, please see any vegetarian or vegan website or consult a nutritionist to find the perfect calculation of protein for you. Results may vary due to size, weight, age, physical condition, and disabilities.

FOOD	PORTION	PROTEIN GRAMS
Almond Milk	8 oz.	1
Almonds	¼ cup	7
Avocados	1	4
Baked Beans (Veg)	1 cup	12
Black Beans	1 cup	11
Broccoli (cooked)	1 cup	4
Brown Rice	1 cup	5
Cottage Cheese	½ cup	14
Egg	1	7
Garbanzo, Kidney Beans	1 cup	15
Garden Burger	1	11
Lentils	1 cup	18
Morningstar Farms Griller	1	15
Peanut Butter	2 T.	8
Peas	½ cup	4
Pinto Beans	1 cup	12
Potato	1 (6 oz.)	4
Quinoa	1 cup	8.14
Seitan	4 oz.	16
Soy Milk	1 cup	8
Spinach	1 cup	5–7
Split Peas	1 cup	16
Sunflower Seeds	¼ cup	6
Tempeh	½ cup	15
Tofu	5 oz.	10.3
Yogurt	6 oz.	7

Appetizers & Hors d'Oeuvres

Baba Ghanoush

Black Olive "Caviar"

Crudités (Raw Veggies and Dip)

Faux Gras Pâté

Feta Tomatoes

Guacamole Dip

Hippie Hummus

Stuffed 'Shrooms

Swiss Cheese Fondue

Vegetarian Gyozas

Baba Ghanoush

Makes 1 cup

1 medium eggplant
½ cup sesame seed oil
⅓ cup lemon juice
1 tablespoon minced garlic
Salt to taste
1 teaspoon cumin
Paprika for garnish
Pita bread, cut into small triangles

Line a broiler toaster oven pan with foil. Spray with nonstick cooking spray. Broil washed and dried eggplant until tender, around 25 minutes. Let cool, then peel carefully.

In a bowl, combine oil, lemon juice, garlic, and salt. Cut the peeled eggplant pulp into small pieces. Add eggplant to the oil and lemon juice mixture and combine well. Pour in batches into the blender. Add cumin and puree for about 90 seconds until it is well blended and has a smooth consistency. If the mixture is too dry, gradually add water one teaspoon at a time and continue on the puree setting until smooth.

Transfer to a glass-covered container. Refrigerate at least one hour or overnight. Sprinkle with paprika and serve with triangles of pita bread.

Black Olive "Caviar"

Makes 2 cups

1 container (12 oz.) cream cheese,
  softened
1 tablespoon cilantro, ground
1 tablespoon parsley flakes
½ teaspoon garlic powder
1 can (4.25 oz.) pitted black olives,
  chopped
Stone-ground seven-grain crackers

This mouth-watering double for caviar is so satisfying. It has the saltiness of caviar without the fish eggs and extravagant expense. Combined with the softened cream cheese and spices, it's a dish you'll want to serve at every party. Serve with champagne whenever possible.

Using a spatula or a blender, combine softened cream cheese with spices until smooth. Scoop the cream cheese mixture into a circular mold in an attractive serving dish. Use a dinner knife to smooth as if you were frosting a cake. Add black olives on top and smooth carefully with the knife. Serve with crackers.

Crudités (Raw Veggies and Dip)

Makes 1 small crudité plate

2 cups baby carrots

1 cup 3-inch celery sticks

1 cup yellow bell peppers, cut in julienne strips

1 cup small broccoli florets

1 cup Blue Cheese or Buttermilk Ranch dressing

This is my go-to appetizer when family and friends come over. Anyone can serve chips and dips, but the elegance and nutrition of the French crudité vegetable dip is absolutely transcendent! Cherry tomatoes, cauliflower, radish rounds, or cucumbers may also be used.

Wash all veggies. Arrange attractively on a serving dish. Add a small dish of dressing or other salad dressing for dipping.

Faux Gras Pâté

Makes 2 cups

2 tablespoons Earth Balance Buttery
    Spread
2 tablespoons black olives, chopped
1 onion, chopped
⅓ cup dry white wine
1 cup button mushrooms, sliced
1 can (15 oz.) garbanzo beans, drained
½ teaspoon soy sauce
2 teaspoons vegetable oil
Salt and pepper to taste
1 teaspoon French tarragon
Sourdough cocktail bread

Foie gras, the fatty French delicacy, is made from the livers of ducks or geese. My vegan version is a satisfying, low-fat, karma-free, and tasty appetizer that can be spread on brioche, cocktail bread, crackers, or pita bread.

Add all ingredients except the French tarragon and bread into a blender. Blend for about 2 minutes. Pour into a decorative bowl and sprinkle tarragon on top. Refrigerate until ready to serve.

Toast bread slices in toaster oven until golden brown, about 4 minutes. Serve on a decorative serving plate.

Feta Tomatoes

Serves 4 to 8

4 red vine-ripe tomatoes
Salt
2 tablespoons Caesar dressing (to make
   your own, see page 79)
4 oz. crumbled feta cheese
2 tablespoons chives, chopped
1 teaspoon paprika

These beautiful tomatoes make an excellent appetizer. The sweetness of ripe tomatoes is combined with the bittersweet taste of Caesar dressing and the rich, smooth taste of feta cheese.

Halve the tomatoes and scoop out seeds and pulp. Add a dash of salt and 1 teaspoon of Caesar dressing to each emptied tomato half. With a fork, further crumble the crumbled feta cheese. Add 1 tablespoon of feta cheese to each tomato half. Sprinkle with chives and paprika. Chill in refrigerator until ready to serve.

Guacamole Dip

Serves 4 to 6

2 avocados, pitted
2 tablespoons green onion, chopped fine
1 ripe tomato, chopped fine
2 tablespoons lime juice, divided
2 tablespoons cilantro, chopped
1 tablespoon garlic powder
1 teaspoon chili powder
Salt and pepper to taste
Chips or crackers

This is an easy homemade guacamole with the taste of Old Mexico. You could add a few tablespoons of salsa and hot sauce, if you like it spicy. If you want it smooth, use a hand blender or a countertop blender. It's simply delicious.

In a medium-size bowl, mash avocados with a fork until smooth. Add onion, tomato, and lime juice. Stir until chunky but smooth, like the consistency of peanut butter. Add cilantro, garlic powder, and chili powder. Add salt and pepper to taste. Combine well. Set aside for one minute.

Rub the interior of the serving bowl with lime. Add guacamole to serving bowl. Serve with chips or crackers.

Hippie Hummus

Makes 2 cups

1 can (15 oz.) garbanzo beans
3 tablespoons lemon juice
1 tablespoon minced garlic
2 tablespoons tahini (sesame butter)
1 teaspoon cumin
1 teaspoon coriander
Salt and pepper to taste
2½ tablespoons garbanzo bean liquid
Pita bread, cut into small triangles

My doctor recently placed me on a low-cholesterol diet. "A minimum of eggs, cheese, butter, and nuts," she said. I found myself eating a lot of Hippie Hummus on seven-grain crackers. It makes a great snack and appetizer with no cholesterol.

Puree all ingredients except bean liquid in blender. If the mixture is too thick and won't move the blades, add water. Open the lid and gradually stir in the bean liquid until mixture becomes smooth. Serve with triangle-cut pieces of pita bread for a Middle East feast.

Stuffed 'Shrooms

Makes 12

12 large fresh mushrooms
1 tablespoon olive oil
2 tablespoons green onions, chopped
    fine
2 tablespoons celery, chopped
1 teaspoon cumin
1 teaspoon parsley flakes
¼ cup breadcrumbs
1 teaspoon water
Salt and pepper to taste

Preheat oven to 350°. Wash mushrooms and remove stems. Place stems in a blender and chop for 2 minutes until fine.

In a skillet, heat oil over medium flame. Sauté onions and celery for 3 minutes. Add mushroom stems, cumin, and parsley. Cook for 3 minutes. Add breadcrumbs and water. Add salt and pepper. Stir and cook 5 minutes. Remove skillet from heat.

With a teaspoon, stuff each mushroom cap carefully with bread mixture. Spray a baking sheet with nonstick cooking spray. Arrange stuffed mushrooms on baking sheet. Bake for 15 minutes. Serve.

This classic Swiss cheese fondue is so easy to make. It's perfect for an elegant party appetizer and has a smooth, light taste to get the meal off to a delicious start. A note on all fondues: if you don't have the fancy fondue pot, you can do the same with a saucepan.

Swiss Cheese Fondue

Serves 8

2 tablespoons minced garlic or garlic spread
1 teaspoon nutmeg
2 cups dry white wine
4 cups Swiss cheese, shredded
1 tablespoon cornstarch
1 tablespoon lemon juice
French bread

Spread garlic all over the interior of the fondue pot. Set aside.

In a medium-size saucepan, cook the nutmeg and half of the wine over medium heat for about 10 minutes. Gradually stir in cheese 1 tablespoon at a time until it has melted into the wine. In a small bowl, combine cornstarch and lemon juice. Stir well and pour into cheese mixture. Stir cheese until smooth and thick. If too thick, add more warm wine. If too thin, add more cornstarch-lemon mixture.

Cut French bread into cubes and arrange on a serving plate. Transfer cheese mixture from saucepan to fondue pot. Heat fondue pot according to instructions. Stir constantly, and dip bread cubes on fondue forks into fondue pot. Voilà.

Vegetarian Gyozas

Makes 24 to 32

GYOZAS

4 tablespoons vegetable oil, divided

1½ cups Morningstar Farms Meal Starter
  Crumbles

1 teaspoon minced garlic

1 cup Chinese Napa or savoy cabbage,
  shredded

1 cup green onions, diced

2 teaspoons mirin (rice wine used for
  cooking)

1 tablespoon soy sauce

2 teaspoons cornstarch, stirred into ¼
  cup water

1 tablespoon ground ginger

1 package gyoza/pot sticker wrappers

DIPPING SAUCE

2 tablespoons soy sauce

1 teaspoon sesame oil

1 tablespoon rice vinegar

1 teaspoon ground ginger

GYOZAS

In a large skillet, heat 1 tablespoon of oil. Add meal starter crumbles and garlic. Sauté for about 5 minutes. Break up the crumbles with a spatula. Remove crumbles mixture from skillet and place in a large bowl. Add cabbage, onions, mirin, and soy sauce to bowl and stir well. Add cornstarch and ginger. Combine well.

Take a gyoza wrapper. With a wet finger, moisten the edges all the way around the wrapper. Place 1 teaspoon of filling in the center of the wrapper. Pick up the wrapper and fold it in half. Press the edges together. Place gyoza on a cutting board and gently crimp the edges with the prongs of a fork. Place gyoza on a plate until ready to fry. Repeat until you have all the gyozas you want to fry.

Spray a large skillet generously with nonstick cooking spray. Add 2 to 3 tablespoons of oil to pan. Heat for 2 minutes until oil sizzles. Add gyozas one at a time. Do not crowd. Fry each side for about 2 minutes, or until golden brown. Remove from skillet and place on a paper towel to dry. To warm before serving, place gyozas in a 375° oven for 5 minutes.

DIPPING SAUCE

Place all ingredients in a glass jar with a lid. Shake jar and pour sauce into a dipping dish to serve.

Morning Foods

Belgian Waffles

French Toast

Groovy Granola

Hatha Yogurt

Irish Oatmeal

Mushroom & Swiss Crepes

One-Egg Omelet

Quiche Deluxe

Swedish Pancakes

Zucchini Pancakes

Belgian Waffles

Makes 12 to 14

3 cups any type of milk

2¼ teaspoons active fast-rising dry yeast

¾ cup unsalted butter, melted

½ cup sugar

3 egg yolks

1 teaspoon vanilla extract

Pinch of salt

3½ cups unbleached flour

3 egg whites

Maple syrup and melted butter
   (optional)

If you don't have a waffle iron or waffle baker, you can use this batter for pancakes. Add ice cream or whipped cream and it's a mouth-watering dessert.

Warm milk in a large bowl. Add yeast. Whisk together and let stand for 5 minutes. Whisk in melted butter, sugar, egg yolks, vanilla, and salt. Gradually add flour. Transfer ingredients from bowl to a blender. Blend until smooth. Pour ingredients back into the bowl. Cover bowl tightly and let batter rise at room temperature for 30 to 60 minutes.

Beat batter again with mixer and fold in egg whites. Beat with mixer a moment.

Lightly spray waffle iron with nonstick cooking spray. Fill each mold with ¼ cup of batter and follow manufacturer's instructions on how long to cook waffles. Remove waffles carefully from molds. Warm syrup and melt butter on top of waffles, if desired, and serve.

French Toast

Serves 4

4 eggs (room temperature)
1 cup low-fat milk
1 tablespoon vanilla extract
4 slices French bread
2 tablespoons butter
2 tablespoons vegetable oil
Confectioner's (powdered) sugar for
    dusting

In a large bowl, whisk eggs, milk, and vanilla. Place bread slices side by side on a large plate or in a baking dish. Pour egg mixture slowly on top of bread slices until they are completely saturated. Soak bread for 10 minutes on each side.

Heat the butter and all the oil in a large skillet over medium heat. Let oil and butter melt completely for 2 minutes. Place soaked bread slices in the skillet. Fry for 5 minutes on each side, or until golden brown. Transfer bread slices with a spatula onto plates. Dust with confectioner's sugar. Serve immediately.

Groovy Granola

Serves 8

3 cups old-fashioned oats
1 cup flaked coconut
2 tablespoons brown sugar
¼ cup honey
¼ teaspoon salt
1 teaspoon vanilla extract
1 tablespoon sunflower oil
1 cup sliced almonds
1 teaspoon cinnamon
1 teaspoon nutmeg
Fresh blueberries (optional)
Milk or yogurt (optional)

I was shopping in a market in the Marin County, California, town of Sausalito a few years ago. My friend and I were searching for granola. I asked a store clerk in which aisle I could find granola. When we looked, there were about sixty different kinds of granola! Now I can make my own granola, and so can you!

Coat a large rimmed cookie sheet with cooking spray. Preheat oven to 350°. In a large bowl, mix together oats and coconut flakes. Transfer to prepared cookie sheet and place in oven. Bake until golden brown, about 45 minutes, stirring every 10 minutes.

Transfer oats and coconut back to a large bowl. Pour in brown sugar, honey, salt, vanilla, oil, almonds, and spices. Combine well and toss to coat all oats well. Spray cookie sheet again with nonstick cooking spray and spread granola evenly on cookie sheet in one layer. Bake for 10 minutes, stir well, and bake for another 10 minutes. Remove cookie sheet from oven and let cool completely.

Transfer granola to a glass or plastic sealed container. Add blueberries, milk and/or plain yogurt for individual portions.

Hatha, in Sanskrit, means "Sun and Moon." Pure and creamy, this yogurt is so easy to make. I like plain yogurt, but if you like it sweet, you can dress it up with vanilla extract or berries.

Hatha Yogurt

Makes 4 cups

4 cups full fat or low-fat milk
Large saucepan with lid
Spatula
A small pan of boiling water
Glass jars with lids
Funnel
⅓ cup yogurt culture*
Whisk

NOTE: Be sure your culture is taken from plain yogurt where the ingredients read, "Made with live active culture."

Preheat oven to 180°. Measure 4 cups of milk into a large saucepan. Turn to low-medium flame. Stir milk with spatula until bubbles begin to form around the edges of the pan. Start a timer for 30 minutes at that point, and continue stirring the milk frequently. Avoid boiling the milk or letting the milk form a brown coat on the bottom of the pan. After 30 minutes, turn off heat, remove saucepan from stove, cover, and let cool for 30 minutes. Stir frequently to avoid that brown buildup on the bottom of the pan.

Meanwhile, start boiling a small pan of water and set aside. Line up the glass jars with lids and a funnel. After 30 minutes, turn off the oven. Get the yogurt culture and whisk it well into the milk mixture. Using a funnel, pour the yogurt carefully into the jars and seal them. Place them on the higher rack in the cooling oven. Place the pan of boiling water beneath the jars on a lower rack in the oven. Let yogurt rest for 8 or 9 hours. Remove jars from oven and refrigerate for at least 4 hours. Serve plain or with fruit.

Irish Oatmeal

Serves 4 to 6

¼ cup brown sugar

3 cups any milk

3½ cups water

1½ cups steel cut oatmeal

Pinch of salt

Maple syrup (optional)

Half-and-half or whipped cream
  (optional)

Pour brown sugar into a baking dish. Press down with a fork to get any lumps out. Set aside.

Bring milk and water to a boil over low heat. Stir in oatmeal and salt. Cook over medium heat for 15 minutes, stirring frequently. Reduce heat and simmer for about 25 minutes. Stir until most of the liquid has been absorbed.

Transfer oatmeal to a microwave-safe baking dish. Sprinkle brown sugar on top of the oatmeal. Place oatmeal in microwave oven on medium for 2 minutes, or place in oven on broil for 2 minutes. Top with maple syrup, half-and-half, or whipped cream.

Mushroom & Swiss Crepes

Serves 4 to 6

Crepes are thin French pancakes—light and lacy, sweet or savory. You can use any filling you'd like, from strawberries and cream to vegetables and beans, but this mushroom and Swiss cheese version is extra deluxe for that Sunday brunch when you cook to impress.

CREPES

3 eggs (room temperature)

½ cup low-fat milk

2 tablespoons unsalted butter, melted

2 tablespoons cold water

Dash of salt

⅓ cup unbleached flour

FILLING

1 tablespoon unsalted butter

3 cups white mushrooms, sliced

1 small red onion, sliced very thin

Salt and pepper to taste

1½ cups Swiss cheese, shredded

4 teaspoons Parmesan cheese, shredded (garnish)

2 tablespoons chives, chopped (garnish)

In a mixing bowl, whisk together eggs, milk, butter, water, and salt. Add flour and whisk until smooth. Let mixture stand for 20 minutes.

Spray a 10-inch crepe skillet with nonstick cooking spray and heat over medium flame for 3 minutes. Stir batter and pour a ¼ cup portion into skillet. Tip and swirl pan so the batter coats the bottom evenly. Cook 40 seconds, flip crepe, and cook the other side for 40 seconds, or until golden brown. Remove crepe from skillet and place on a paper towel. Respray skillet and repeat 3 times, respraying the skillet each time and letting the crepes rest over one another on top of paper towels.

Spray the skillet with cooking spray. Add butter and cook over medium flame 1 minute. Add mushrooms and onions. Sauté for 7 minutes. Add salt and pepper and remove from heat. While still steaming, add the Swiss cheese and stir gently.

Place 1 crepe on a serving plate. Spoon in 1/4 of the mushroom-cheese mixture. Roll the crepe like a burrito and place on a plate, seam side down. Garnish with Parmesan and chives.

This is a quick and simple way to make breakfast without all the fuss. You can dress this omelet up with cheese, mushrooms, and tomatoes or just about anything if you have the time.

One-Egg Omelet

Makes 1

2 teaspoons butter or margarine
1 egg
2 tablespoons low-fat milk
½ teaspoon parsley flakes
Pinch salt and pepper

Spray skillet with nonstick cooking spray. Turn on low flame and add butter or margarine. Turn skillet to coat carefully with it. Do not let the butter brown.

In a small bowl, crack the egg and add milk, parsley, salt, and pepper. Whisk well. Add egg mixture to skillet and let cook for 2 minutes over low heat, tilting the pan and moving it around so all sides of the omelet are cooked. Cover pan for 1 minute. Uncover pan and gently pry the edges of the egg mixture with a spatula. Carefully fold omelet over so it resembles a burrito, then gently flip it over. Cover and cook 1 minute more.

Remove from pan and plate.

Quiche Deluxe
Serves 8 to 10

1 deep-dish pie crust
¼ stick unsalted butter
1 cup green onions, chopped fine
4 cups button mushrooms, sliced
1 teaspoon parsley
Salt and pepper to taste
4 eggs (room temperature)
½ cup low-fat milk
½ cup fat-free half-and-half
1 teaspoon nutmeg
1½ cups cheddar cheese, grated
1 tablespoon imitation bacon bits
⅓ cup Parmesan cheese, shredded

This French traditional quiche is like a big omelet pie. I have cut down on the fat content by using fat-free half-and-half and low-fat milk. Impress your friends and family. This is perfect for a breakfast or brunch dish. Bon appétit!

Preheat oven to 450°. Bake pie crust for 15 minutes. Remove pie crust from oven and set aside. Reduce oven temperature to 400°.

In a large skillet, melt butter over medium flame. Add onions and sauté for 2 minutes. Add mushrooms and stir. Sauté for 5 minutes. Sprinkle with parsley, salt, and pepper. Remove skillet from heat and set aside. In large bowl, whisk eggs, milk, and half-and-half together. Add nutmeg, 1 cup of cheddar cheese, and the mushroom mixture.

Pour filling into pie crust. Top with remaining cheddar cheese, imitation bacon bits, and Parmesan cheese. Bake until golden brown, about 50 minutes. Insert a toothpick in the center. If it comes out clean, it's done. Cut into wedges and serve.

Have you ever been to the River Inn Restaurant in Guerneville, California? It's on the Russian River, about sixty miles north of San Francisco. Their Swedish pancakes are legendary! This is my version. Not bad at all.

Swedish Pancakes

Serves 4

4 eggs
2 cups low-fat milk
½ cup unbleached flour, sifted
1 tablespoon brown sugar
2 tablespoons butter, melted (and more to top pancakes)
Maple syrup (optional)

Whisk eggs well in a large bowl. Add milk, flour, brown sugar, and butter. Whisk for 1 minute and then turn hand mixer to medium speed and blend for 3 minutes, or until batter is smooth.

Spray a large skillet with nonstick cooking spray. Heat on high for 1 minute. Restir batter and pour about ¼ cup into the center of the skillet. Reduce heat to medium and cook for about 2½ minutes. Flip pancake over with a large spatula. You should see a brown design like rain puddles with taffeta patterns. Cook the other side about 2½ minutes. Using a spatula, transfer pancakes from skillet to plates.

Respray the skillet with cooking spray for each pancake and follow the same directions. Top with butter and maple syrup, if using. Plate.

Zucchini Pancakes

Makes 18 to 24

3 zucchini squashes
1 carrot
3 eggs, beaten
5 tablespoons unbleached flour
3 tablespoons Parmesan cheese
1 tablespoon parsley flakes
1 teaspoon garlic powder
1 teaspoon paprika
Salt and pepper to taste
2 tablespoons cooking oil
Sour cream (optional)

Finely grate zucchini and carrot into a large bowl. Add eggs, flour, Parmesan, seasonings, salt, and pepper. Spray a large skillet liberally with cooking spray. Add oil and heat over low flame for 1 minute. Increase heat to medium.

Drop batter in tablespoon-size portions into skillet. Cook for 4 minutes, flip pancake, and cook for 4 minutes on the other side. Use a plastic spatula to check and see if they are golden brown. Remove pancake carefully from skillet, place on a paper towel, and keep warm.

Serve with a dollop of sour cream, if using, and a sprinkle of parsley flakes. Keep frying pancakes until all the batter is gone.

Soups

Celery Cream

Chickpea Noodle

French Cream of Mushroom

¡Gazpacho Gustavo!

Laurel Canyon Lentil Stew

Mellow Yellow Split Pea

Sweet Corn Chowder

Tomato Velvet Cream

Very Veggie Broth

Vichyssoise

Celery Cream

Serves 8

¼ cup unsalted butter
8 stalks celery, diced
1 cup green onions, diced
1 cup cauliflower, chopped
¼ cup unbleached flour
4 cups vegetable broth (I recommend my
   Very Veggie Broth, see page 71)
2 tablespoons dry white wine
1 tablespoon parsley flakes
1 teaspoon oregano
1 cup milk
Salt and pepper to taste
1 tablespoon chives, chopped (garnish)

When I was a child, my favorite Campbell soup was Cream of Celery. This version of the soup includes cauliflower, white wine, and oregano. These savory additions bring out the exquisite flavor of celery.

In a soup pot, melt butter. Stir in celery, onions, and cauliflower. Cook 10 minutes over low heat. Stir in flour and bring to a boil. Add broth, wine, parsley, and oregano. Reduce heat and simmer 10 minutes, or until all vegetables are tender.

Pour soup in batches into a blender or use a hand blender. Puree 1 minute each. Return soup to pot. Stir in milk. Heat on medium high. Do not boil. Add salt and pepper. Garnish with chopped chives.

Chickpea Noodle

Serves 4 to 6

5 cups vegetable broth (I recommend my
   Very Veggie Broth, see page 71)
1½ cups water
1 cup yellow onions, diced fine
2 tablespoons green onions, sliced fine
1 cup carrots, sliced
1½ cups celery, chopped fine
1 can (15 oz.) chickpeas and liquid
1 teaspoon soy sauce
1 teaspoon garlic powder
1 tablespoon parsley flakes
Salt and pepper to taste
2 cups Manischewitz medium egg
   noodles

Chicken noodle soup has been called the Jewish penicillin. When you were sick, Mom always gave you chicken noodle soup—the ultimate comfort food. Now you don't have to sacrifice taste in order to enjoy this vegetarian version. I have replaced the chicken with chickpeas, and the chicken broth with a hearty vegetable broth. Chickpea Noodle Soup satisfies. No guilt trips, clean karma, and a healthy, delicious taste.

In a large pot, heat broth, water, onions, carrots, and celery over medium heat for 5 minutes. Partly cover the pot with a lid. Add chickpeas and liquid. Stir in soy sauce. Add seasonings, salt, and pepper and let the mixture come to a boil. Stir and reduce heat simmering for 10 minutes. Add egg noodles and heat, on low for 10 minutes. Turn off heat. Let soup rest, covered, for 10 minutes. Taste and adjust seasonings.

French Cream of Mushroom

Serves 4 to 6

1 tablespoon unsalted butter

1 tablespoon olive oil

1 yellow onion, chopped

3 celery stalks, chopped

2 cups white button mushrooms, sliced

½ cup dry white wine

5 cups vegetable broth (I recommend my Very Veggie Broth, see page 71)

2 small potatoes, peeled and cut into cubes

¾ cup milk

1 teaspoon herbes de Provence

Salt and pepper to taste

Tucked away on a small Paris street is a tiny French bistro. The café curtains are open and the smells of herbs, sautéed onions, and freshly baked bread gently waft through the air. Here is a soup inspired by this French experience.

Heat a large saucepan over medium heat. Add butter and olive oil. Stir in onion and celery, and sauté for 5 minutes. Stir in mushrooms and sauté for 10 minutes. Add wine and vegetable broth. Bring to a boil. Add potatoes. Cover pan and simmer for 15 minutes, until potatoes are soft but not mushy. Remove soup from heat and let cool for 20 minutes.

With a slotted spoon, remove 3 tablespoons of the vegetables and set aside. Puree soup with a blender or hand blender until well blended. Return soup to pan. Stir in milk, herbs, salt, and pepper. Return vegetable bits to the soup pan. Reheat gently. Do not let it come to a boil before serving.

¡Gazpacho Gustavo!

Serves 4 to 6

3 tomatoes, chopped coarsely
1 cucumber, peeled and sliced
1½ cups celery, chopped
1 red bell pepper, seeded and chopped
4 cups tomato juice
¼ cup red wine vinegar
1 tablespoon olive oil
1 teaspoon red cocktail sauce
1 teaspoon lemon juice
Chives and cilantro, chopped fine

I went to the Hollywood Bowl and saw the young Venezuelan-born conductor Gustavo Dudamel conduct the L.A. Philharmonic Orchestra. I was blown away! I was so impressed with him that I named this gazpacho after him.

In a blender, combine tomatoes, cucumber, celery, bell pepper, tomato juice, red wine vinegar, and oil. Puree for 1 minute. Pour mixture into a glass jar with a lid or a sealed pitcher. Stir in cocktail sauce and lemon juice. Chill in refrigerator for one hour or overnight. Garnish with chives and cilantro.

Laurel Canyon Lentil Stew

Serves 6

High in protein and vitamins, this Canyon version of the old favorite is satisfying and delicious anytime you serve it.

5 cups water
1½ cups brown lentils
1 cup purple onion, diced
¼ teaspoon salt
½ cup carrots, chopped
1 teaspoon cumin
1 teaspoon minced garlic
2 tablespoons tomato paste
3 ripe tomatoes, diced
1 teaspoon chives, chopped
1 teaspoon soy sauce

"When Jacob had cooked stew, Esau came in from the field and he was famished; and Esau said to Jacob, "Please let me have a swallow of that red stuff there, for I am famished." But Jacob said, "First sell me your birthright." Esau said, "Behold, I am about to die, so of what use then is the birthright to me?" And Jacob said, "First swear to me." So he swore to him, and sold his birthright to Jacob. Then Jacob gave Esau bread and lentil stew; and he ate and drank, and rose and went on his way." —Genesis 25:29-34

In a large pot, boil water. While it's heating, rinse and drain lentils. Add lentils, onion, salt, carrots, cumin, and garlic to boiled water. Simmer on low heat, covered, for 1 hour, stirring every 10 minutes. Stir in tomato paste, tomatoes, chives, and soy sauce. Simmer, covered, on low heat for another 30 minutes. Stir, and ladle into serving bowls.

Mellow Yellow Split Pea

Serves 4 to 6

1 cup yellow split peas
5 cups water (for simmering yellow split peas)
½ cup yellow onions, chopped
½ cup celery, chopped
½ cup carrots, chopped fine
⅓ cup frozen corn
6 cups water
1 teaspoon each of garlic powder, salt, pepper, parsley flakes, and cilantro
Paprika (garnish)

This soup is a tribute to my favorite male singer, Donovan. This soup is so nutritious and has a mellow taste with plenty of protein.

Rinse and drain yellow split peas. Add 5 cups of water and bring to a boil in a large pot. Simmer for 1 hour. Add all vegetables and 6 cups of water. Bring to a boil. Add seasonings and simmer for 1 hour. Taste to see if peas are soft. If not, keep simmering another 20 minutes. Garnish with paprika and serve.

Sweet Corn Chowder

Serves 4 to 6

1½ tablespoons unsalted butter
1 yellow onion, chopped
Pinch of salt and pepper
1 package (12 oz.) frozen sweet corn,
    cooked and divided
1 large russet potato
2 cups vegetable broth (I recommend my
    Very Veggie Broth, see page 71)
1¼ cups milk
Basil, cilantro, and chives (garnish)

This classic soup is good any time of the year. Add pumpkin spice or paprika for a spicier, more colorful version.

Melt butter over medium heat in a pot. Sauté onions with salt and pepper for 15 to 20 minutes, or until golden brown. Cook bag of frozen corn per package instructions. Let corn cool while you peel and cube the potato and set aside. Reserve ¾ cup of corn kernels and ½ cup of potato cubes and set aside.

Add vegetable broth, remaining corn, and potatoes to soup pot. Simmer on medium heat for 15 minutes, covered. Add milk and stir well. Remove from heat and puree in a blender 1 cup at a time until it's as smooth as silk. Return soup to pot and add remaining corn and potatoes. Simmer on low heat for 20 minutes. Do not let boil. Garnish with basil, cilantro, and chives.

Tomato Velvet Cream

Serves 4

1 tablespoon sunflower oil

1 small purple onion, diced

5 celery stalks, diced

1 tablespoon minced garlic

1 teaspoon cumin

1 teaspoon ground coriander

1 can (14 oz.) diced tomatoes, including liquid

1 can (6 oz.) tomato paste

1 cup milk

1 tablespoon basil

1 teaspoon garlic powder

Salt and pepper to taste

1 tablespoon parsley flakes (add more for garnish)

There's something so satisfying about a bowl of tomato soup. With a grilled cheese sandwich, it's the all-American meatless meal for lunch or dinner. Try it for a Meatless Monday.

In a large saucepan, heat oil for 1 minute. Sauté onion, celery, garlic, cumin, and coriander over medium heat for 5 minutes. Transfer onion mixture to a blender, along with diced tomatoes, and blend for 2 minutes. Transfer blender mixture back to saucepan. Cook on medium flame until boiling, lower heat, and stir in tomato paste. Slowly stir in milk and remaining seasonings. Simmer on low heat. Do not boil. Turn off heat. Garnish with parsley flakes and serve.

Very Veggie Broth

Makes 2 quarts

2 quarts water

4 celery stalks, chopped

2 carrots, chopped

10 cherry tomatoes, halved

1½ cups red onion, chopped

10 white button mushrooms, chopped, including stems

1 zucchini, sliced

2 potatoes, sliced

1 teaspoon each of coriander, cumin, and paprika

This vegetable broth makes an excellent base for any soup. When I chop vegetables for casseroles or salads, I place all the scraps, even potato peels, into a sealed plastic bag and pop it in the freezer. When I need vegetable broth, I use this recipe.

Heat 2 quarts of water. Place vegetables and seasonings into the pot, and let it boil. Simmer for 45 minutes on lowest heat. Turn off heat, and let the broth cool. Strain well. Discard vegetables. Pour liquid into a sealed container, if storing. It will keep 3 days in the refrigerator, or 3 months in the freezer.

You can use whatever types and quantities of vegetables you'd like. I have compiled this recipe for a seven-vegetable broth, but you could certainly add more or less according to your taste. You could add 2 tablespoons of soy sauce and/or 1 tablespoon of tomato paste to give the broth a flavor and color boost.

Vichyssoise

Serves 6 to 8

1 tablespoon unsalted butter
2 leeks, cleaned and sliced
4 celery stalks, chopped
½ tablespoon minced garlic
¼ cup dry white wine
8 small Yukon potatoes
4½ cups water
1 pink shallot, coarsely diced
¾ cup light sour cream
¼ teaspoon salt
Dash of pepper
1 tablespoon French tarragon
2 tablespoons chives, finely chopped
  (garnish)

This French classic potato-leek soup may be served warm or cold. It may be thinned out with water, as it tends to puff up like mashed potatoes after pureeing it.

In a soup pot, melt butter on medium heat. Add leeks, celery, and garlic. Stir, cover, and reduce heat. Simmer 10 minutes until leeks are tender. Stir in wine and cook 5 minutes. Peel and dice potatoes into small cubes. Stir in potatoes, water, and shallot. Cover and reduce heat to low. Simmer 30 minutes until potatoes are soft.

Cool soup for 10 minutes. Puree in batches in a blender until smooth, or use a hand blender. Stir in sour cream, salt, pepper, and tarragon. Garnish with chives.

Salads and Dressings

Asian Autumn Salad

Caesar Salad

Chinese Chickpea Salad

Cranberry Collage Salad

Israeli Salad

French Salad Niçoise

Le Cobb & French Dressing

Waldorf Astoria Salad

"We Got the Beet" Salad

Asian Autumn Salad with Dressing

Serves 4 to 6

SALAD

2 cups romaine lettuce, shredded

2 cups red cabbage, shredded

1 cup button mushrooms, sliced

3 stalks celery, sliced diagonally

2 green onion stalks, sliced fine

2 large navel oranges, peeled and cut into pieces

2 cups mung bean sprouts

1 teaspoon ground ginger

1 teaspoon garlic powder

Salt and pepper to taste

DRESSING

2 tablespoons sesame oil

2 tablespoons rice vinegar

1 teaspoon lemon juice

1 tablespoon soy sauce

2 tablespoons tahini

½ teaspoon ground ginger

½ teaspoon onion powder

1 tablespoon honey

1 teaspoon minced garlic

Salt and pepper to taste

This tasty Asian salad has it all—sweet and sour, salty and tangy, and the orange and ginger give it just the right Asian flair to rival your favorite Chinese take-out restaurant, but without the MSG. This recipe was featured in Vegetarian Times *magazine's September 2011 issue in the Reader Recipe column.*

SALAD

Add all the salad ingredients into a large bowl and combine, tossing gently.

DRESSING

Place all ingredients in a small glass jar with a lid. Close lid and shake vigorously. Adjust seasonings to taste. Refrigerate until ready to serve. Serve on the side, or pour over salad and toss.

Caesar Salad with Dressing

Serves 4 to 6

DRESSING

½ cup mayonnaise or vegan mayonnaise

½ cup plain yogurt (to make your own, see page 39)

⅓ cup low-fat milk

1 tablespoon red wine vinegar

1 teaspoon ground mustard

1½ teaspoons lemon juice

3 tablespoons Parmesan cheese

1 teaspoon minced garlic

Salt and pepper to taste

SALAD

1 head romaine lettuce

½ cup grated Parmesan cheese

CROUTONS

4 slices French sourdough bread

3 tablespoons melted ghee (clarified butter)

1 teaspoon garlic powder

1 teaspoon herbes de Provence seasoning

DRESSING

Pour all ingredients into glass jar with a lid, cover, and shake until blended. Refrigerate until ready to serve.

SALAD

Lay lettuce leaves out horizontally and cut into fourths. Arrange leaves in a large, chilled salad bowl.

CROUTONS

Preheat a skillet on medium heat. Cut bread into cubes. Melt ghee in skillet. In a small bowl, add the bread cubes and sasonings. Coat all bread cubes well with seasonings. Add bread cubes to the skillet and fry for 2 minutes on each side, turning the croutons once. Remove croutons from heat and drain on a paper towel. Set aside to cool before tossing them, along with cheese and dressing, into the salad.

Chinese Chickpea Salad

Serves 4

1 head romaine or Boston lettuce, cut in
    pieces
1 can (15 oz.) chickpeas, drained well
3 celery stalks, sliced diagonally
6 large white button mushrooms, sliced
    thin
⅓ cup green onions, sliced fine
1 large navel orange, peeled and sliced in
    pieces
1 cup mung bean sprouts
Salt and pepper to taste
¾ cup Asian Dressing (see Asian
    Autumn Salad, page 77)
1 teaspoon cumin
½ teaspoon ground ginger
½ cup sliced almonds

Try this simply delicious variation on the classic Chinese chicken salad. I have replaced the chicken with chickpeas and added some surprises like mushrooms and sliced almonds. The Asian Dressing from the Asian Autumn Salad goes well with this salad. All the tastes you love—sweet, sour, salty, and crunchy!

In a large salad bowl, combine lettuce, chickpeas, celery, mushrooms, green onions, and orange slices. Toss well. Add bean sprouts, salt, and pepper. Toss again. Refrigerate while you make the Asian Dressing. Refrigerate dressing before serving. Pour onto salad and mix well. Add spices and sliced almonds, and mix again before plating.

Cranberry Collage Salad

Serves 6 to 8

1 package (5 oz.) Baby Greens salad
4 cups mixed arugula and radicchio
1½ cups chopped walnuts
2 tablespoons brown sugar
2 tablespoons unsalted butter
2 tablespoons water
1 teaspoon nutmeg
1 package (6 oz.) dried cranberries
4 oz. crumbled blue cheese
½ cup balsamic vinaigrette

Here's a delicious new gourmet way to serve cranberries at Thanksgiving or anytime. The crunchy walnuts and tangy blue cheese really wake up your taste buds. Or add pear slices for the Christmas holidays.

Arrange the Baby Greens, arugula, and radicchio attractively in a large salad bowl and refrigerate.

Preheat oven to 400°. Spray an aluminum baking sheet with nonstick cooking spray. Pour walnuts onto prepared cookie sheet. Cover walnuts with brown sugar, butter, water, and nutmeg. Bake for 5 minutes. Remove candied walnuts from oven, strain, and cool for 10 minutes.

Add dried cranberries to salad bowl. Stir in candied walnuts and blue cheese crumbles. Arrange colorfully. Top with balsamic vinaigrette and toss gently.

French Salad Niçoise with Lemon Vinaigrette

Serves 6 to 8

SALAD

3 small red or white rose potatoes

2 eggs

2 cups spinach, washed and dried

2 cups romaine lettuce, cut into strips

1 cup canned white beans, drained

1 tomato, cut into wedges

1 cup black olives, sliced

2 cups French-style green beans

1 cup white mushrooms, sliced

4 celery stalks, diced fine

5 green onions, diced (set aside 2
tablespoons for garnish)

DRESSING

¼ cup lemon juice

⅓ cup olive oil

1 teaspoon Dijon mustard

1 teaspoon red wine vinegar

1 teaspoon ground basil

1 teaspoon parsley flakes

½ teaspoon minced garlic

Salt and pepper to taste

This is a hearty and satisfying vegetarian version of the classic French salad. I've replaced the tuna with white beans and mushrooms. Feel free to add avocado and red bell pepper.

Place potatoes in a saucepan with water to cover. Simmer over medium heat until boiling. Reduce heat and cook for 4 minutes. Remove potatoes from stove and let cool. Add eggs to boiled water and cook on medium heat for 8 minutes. Turn off heat and cover eggs for 5 minutes. Peel eggs carefully, slice into rounds, and set aside.

Make dressing by placing lemon juice, oil, mustard, vinegar, and the seasonings in a glass jar with a lid. Cover jar tightly with lid and shake. Refrigerate jar.

Drain, cool, and dice potatoes. Place in a bowl. Set aside. Arrange spinach and lettuce around the rim of a large salad bowl. Add white beans, tomato, olives, potatoes, eggs, and green beans in separate sections of the bowl. Arrange mushrooms, celery, and green onions each in sections. Top with green onions. Pour shaken dressing over each individual portion.

Israeli Salad

Serves 4

SALAD

2 tomatoes, chopped fine

3 green onions, diced fine

3 celery stalks, chopped fine

1 cucumber, peeled, seeded, and chopped
  fine

1 orange bell pepper, seeded and diced
  fine

½ cup carrots, sliced thin

Salt to taste

1 ripe avocado, pitted and diced

LEMON VINAIGRETTE DRESSING

¼ cup lemon juice

1 tablespoon olive oil

1 teaspoon red wine vinegar

1 teaspoon dill weed

Dash of coriander and French tarragon

1 teaspoon minced garlic

Salt and pepper to taste

In a large salad bowl, combine vegetables (except avocado). Sprinkle with salt and refrigerate. In a separate small glass jar with a lid, combine lemon juice, oil, vinegar, and seasonings. Cover tightly and shake well. Refrigerate. When ready to serve, pour dressing from jar over chopped vegetables in large salad bowl. Add avocado pieces. Toss gently before serving.

Le Cobb Salad with French Dressing

Serves 4

DRESSING

⅓ cup vegetable oil

1 tablespoon dry white wine

½ teaspoon horseradish

Salt and pepper to taste

⅓ cup ketchup

1 teaspoon paprika

½ teaspoon minced garlic

1 tablespoon French tarragon

3 tablespoons red wine vinegar

1 tablespoon dry white wine

1 tablespoon lemon juice

½ teaspoon Dijon mustard

SALAD

3 eggs

1 head romaine lettuce

7 slices MorningStar Farms Bacon Strips

1 package (10 oz.) Gardein Chick'n Strips

⅓ cup green onions, diced

1 large ripe avocado, sliced

12 cherry tomatoes

1 cup crumbled blue cheese

Salt and pepper to taste

Basil leaves (garnish)

The Hollywood legend goes something like this: Brown Derby restaurant proprietor Bob Cobb had Grauman's Chinese Theatre owner Sid Grauman in his restaurant late one evening in 1937. The chefs had gone home, so Cobb threw whatever he had on hand from the refrigerator into a bowl, added French dressing, and created the Cobb Salad. The rest is history.

DRESSING

Combine all French dressing ingredients in a large covered jar. Shake and refrigerate.

SALAD

Hard-boil eggs, then peel, halve, and set aside. Arrange lettuce in the bottom of serving bowls. In a skillet, fry "bacon" strips and Gardein Chick'n Strips per package instructions (use nonstick cooking spray). Let "bacon" and "chick'n" drain and cool on a paper towel. Dice green onions. Place onions over avocado and lettuce. Arrange "bacon" strips, chick'n" strips, halved eggs, cherry tomatoes, and blue cheese in separate sections in salad bowls. Sprinkle with salt and pepper. Garnish with basil leaves. Serve chilled French dressing on the side.

Waldorf Astoria Salad

Serves 4

8 Boston lettuce leaves
1 large green apple, diced, with skin on
1 tablespoon lemon juice
1 cup celery, chopped
1 ripe yellow pear, peeled and diced
2 cups seedless purple grapes
1½ cups walnut pieces
Dash of salt
¾ cup mayonnaise

This traditional New York fruit salad has the versatility to go with any meal from breakfast to a Thanksgiving feast.

Drape a large bowl or four separate salad bowls with lettuce leaves. Set aside. In a large bowl, mix apples and lemon juice. Add celery, pear, grapes, walnuts, and salt. Stir in mayonnaise until well combined and well coated. Chill. Pour mixture over lettuce leaves.

"We Got the Beet" Salad

Serves 6 to 8

DRESSING

3 tablespoons olive oil

2 tablespoons balsamic vinegar

1 teaspoon lemon juice

1 teaspoon ground mustard

1 teaspoon garlic powder

1 cup black walnut pieces

1 tablespoon water

1 teaspoon sugar

SALAD

1 package (5 oz.) Baby Spring Salad
   greens

1 can (15 oz.) beets, sliced and drained

1 cup crumbled feta cheese

Salt and pepper to taste

In a small glass jar with a lid, combine oil, vinegar, lemon juice, mustard, and garlic powder. Screw lid on tightly and shake well. Refrigerate jar.

In a small skillet over medium heat, cook walnuts in water and sugar for 3 minutes. Set aside and let cool.

In a large salad bowl, combine greens and dressing. Coat salad leaves well. Divide into salad bowls. Top each serving with beets, feta cheese, salt, pepper, and walnuts.

Side Dishes

Chana Masala

Chanukah Potato Latkes

Duchess Potatoes

French Carrots

Fried Green Tomatoes

Golden Cauliflower

Mexican Red Pinto Beans

Roquefort Potatoes au Gratin

Yellow Corn Muffins

Yorkshire Pudding Puffs

Chana Masala

Serves 4

2 tablespoons olive oil

2 tablespoons ghee (clarified butter)

1 onion, chopped

5 celery stalks, diced

1 can (15.5 oz.) chickpeas, drained and
    rinsed

1 tablespoon lemon juice

2 large tomatoes, diced

½ cup frozen baby peas

⅓ cup water

1 teaspoon garam masala

1 teaspoon cumin

1 teaspoon curry powder

½ teaspoon turmeric

In this classic dish from India, the warm Indian spices are added last rather than cooked first. Here the warm golds, yellows, and browns can be seen in a more impressive light. The ghee gives the dish a nutty sweetness that's incredible.

Heat the oil and ghee in a skillet over medium flame. Add the onion and celery. Sauté until translucent. Continue to sauté for another 5 minutes.

Stir in the chickpeas, lemon juice, tomatoes, peas, and ⅓ cup of water. Bring to a simmer, then cover and cook over medium-low heat for 8 minutes. Stir well, adding water as needed so it does not become too dry. Remove from heat and top with spices. Serve over a bed of hot basmati rice.

Chanukah Potato Latkes

Serves 6 to 8

6 potatoes
3 tablespoons olive oil
¾ cup yellow onions, diced
½ cup green onions, diced
2 tablespoons flour, sifted
½ cup cheese, grated
3 tablespoons low-fat milk
1 egg, beaten
2 teaspoons paprika
Salt and pepper
1 cup light sour cream
3 tablespoons chives, diced

The festival of Chanukah is all about the oil. Do not skimp on the oil. Use as much as you need to create these golden brown potato pancakes. Double or triple this recipe if you are cooking for a crowd or eating the latkes for eight nights. L' Chaim!

Boil the water in a large pot over medium heat. Peel potatoes, cut into small pieces, and add to the pot. Cover the pot and steam for 20 minutes.

Heat oil in a skillet and sauté onions until brown, 5 to 8 minutes. Turn off heat and set onions aside. Check potatoes. You want them soft but not mushy. Insert a knife into the potatoes and if it comes out smoothly, they are done. Drain and mash potatoes in a large bowl. Add green onions, flour, cheese, and milk. Combine and stir the batter. Add egg and seasonings and mix well.

In a separate large skillet, cook oil on medium flame. Form potato mixture into small pancakes and drop into the oiled skillet. Fry latkes in batches, about 3 minutes per side, until golden brown. Drain on paper towels. Serve with a dollop of sour cream and a sprinkle of chives on top.

Mashed potatoes are an all-American comfort food, but when you want to make an impression with mashed potatoes, you want to serve Duchess Potatoes. The French flair of the small potato puffs will add an elegant touch to the meal. Get fancy with a pastry bag and make rosettes, stars, crescents, or any shape or size you'd like.

Duchess Potatoes

Serves 6

8 small Yukon Gold potatoes
Salted water
½ cup milk, divided
3 tablespoons butter
2 egg yolks
1 teaspoon lemon juice
Salt and pepper
1 teaspoon minced garlic

Peel and cut potatoes in small pieces. Cook potatoes in a saucepan, with enough salted water to just cover potatoes, for 20 minutes or until tender. Remove potatoes from heat and drain. Return potatoes to saucepan.

Mash potatoes with a masher until they are smooth without lumps. Add ¼ cup of the milk, butter, and egg yolks. Stir well. Add lemon juice, salt, pepper, and garlic. Stir in remaining ¼ cup of milk. Potatoes should be smooth but stiff.

Spray a baking sheet with nonstick cooking spray. Spoon the potato mixture onto baking sheet with a teaspoon. With the tines of a fork, press onto potato mounds to make striped marks. To bake later on, cover cookie sheet with foil and refrigerate up to 24 hours. To bake now, preheat oven to 400°. Bake for 20 minutes or until golden brown.

French Carrots
Serves 6

4 cups carrots, sliced into rounds
4 tablespoons butter or margarine
1 cup orange juice
1 teaspoon parsley flakes
1 teaspoon French tarragon
Salt and pepper to taste

In a large skillet, sauté carrots in butter for 7 minutes. Add orange juice and parsley. Cook over medium flame until carrots are tender, about 15 minutes. Drain carrots well. Sprinkle with tarragon, salt, and pepper.

Fried Green Tomatoes
Serves 6

6 green tomatoes
2 large eggs
¼ cup milk
¾ cup flour
1 cup cornmeal
1 cup breadcrumbs
½ cup olive oil
Salt and pepper

Slice tomatoes into half-inch-thick slices. Whisk eggs and milk in a small bowl. Pour flour onto a plate. Mix together cornmeal and breadcrumbs in a large bowl. Dip tomato slices first in flour to coat. Dip tomato slices second into egg mixture, and then dredge them in breadcrumbs mixture. Dust off the excess breadcrumbs from tomato slices.

Pour oil into a large skillet heating over medium flame. Place tomatoes in skillet 4 at a time, and fry for 5 minutes on each side until golden brown. Drain and serve.

Golden Cauliflower
Serves 6

1 head cauliflower
4 tablespoons olive oil
2 teaspoons minced garlic
2 teaspoons turmeric
1 teaspoon cumin
1 teaspoon curry powder
Salt and pepper to taste

Preheat oven to 350°. Place cauliflower head into a baking dish. In a skillet, heat oil. Add garlic. Cook 3 minutes. Pour oil mixture over cauliflower so it is well coated. Bake cauliflower 35 minutes in a baking dish until golden. Sprinkle with turmeric, cumin, curry, salt, and pepper. Serve in a decorative bowl.

Mexican Red Pinto Beans

Serves 6

1 tablespoon butter
1 yellow onion, chopped very fine
1 teaspoon minced garlic
1 teaspoon oregano
1 teaspoon chili powder
1 teaspoon cumin
Salt and pepper to taste
2 cans (15 oz. each) pinto beans, drained
2 cups water
1 jar (10 oz.) spaghetti sauce
¼ cup light brown sugar

Heat butter in a large pot over medium flame. Sauté onions for 5 minutes. Add garlic, oregano, chili powder, cumin, salt, and pepper. Cook for 2 minutes. Add pinto beans and water. Cover and heat to boiling. Reduce heat and simmer for 45 minutes. Stir well.

Add spaghetti sauce and brown sugar. Heat to boiling. Reduce heat and simmer 20 minutes. Serve over Yellow Corn Muffins (see page 109), if desired.

Roquefort Potatoes au Gratin

Serves 4

1 teaspoon garlic powder

6 red potatoes, peeled and sliced in ¼-inch rounds

1 red onion, sliced into rings

3 tablespoons unsalted melted butter

3 tablespoons flour

1 teaspoon nutmeg

2 cups low-fat milk

⅓ cup crumbled Roquefort (blue) cheese

1 teaspoon paprika

Potatoes get all dressed up with Roquefort (blue cheese) in this tasty side dish. Give your table a gourmet European flair. Perfect for a dinner party or a holiday meal.

Preheat oven to 400°. Spray a glass casserole dish with nonstick cooking spray. Sprinkle with garlic powder. Layer half of the potato slices on the bottom of the casserole dish. Top with onion slices and remaining potato slices.

In a small saucepan, melt butter over low heat. Add flour, nutmeg, and stir in milk slowly. Stir until mixture thickens, about 5 minutes. Stir in Roquefort cheese until melted, about 1 minute. Pour milk/cheese mixture over the potatoes. Sprinkle with paprika. Cover with aluminum foil. Bake 1 hour. Remove foil and serve.

Yellow Corn Muffins

Makes 20 muffins

1½ cups unbleached flour

⅔ cup sugar

½ cup cornmeal

Dash of salt

1 tablespoon baking powder

1½ cups milk

2 eggs, beaten

¼ cup vegetable oil

½ cup frozen corn, thawed

3 tablespoons unsalted butter

I made these easy muffins for a Thanksgiving dinner. Everyone raved about them. The corn kernels really help. These muffins go well with any meal, and for sopping up gravy, they are indispensable.

Preheat oven to 350°. Spray muffin pan cups generously with nonstick cooking spray. In a large bowl, combine all dry ingredients. In another bowl, whisk together milk, eggs, oil, thawed corn, and butter. Pour wet ingredients into flour mixture bowl. Stir well.

Fill each muffin tin cup ⅔ full. Bake 20 to 25 minutes until toothpick test comes out clean. Cool 10 minutes. When done, invert muffin tin pan. Serve.

Yorkshire Pudding Puffs

Serves 6 to 8

3 eggs, beaten
1 cup low-fat milk
2 cups unbleached flour
½ teaspoon nutmeg
Salt and pepper to taste
2 tablespoons unsalted butter

Yorkshire Pudding is usually served with Prime Rib, but for Vegetarians, it can be served just about any time. They are a cross between a roll and a biscuit. Perfect for Holiday meals like Thanksgiving and Christmas. Ideal with mushroom gravy.

Preheat oven to 375°. In a large mixing bowl, whisk eggs and milk until well combined. Add flour, nutmeg, salt, and pepper to the bowl. Beat with a mixer for 2 minutes on medium speed until smooth. Set aside.

Spray a 12-cup muffin tin with nonstick cooking spray. Add ½ teaspoon of butter to each cup. Place sprayed and buttered muffin tin in the oven and bake for 3 minutes. Remove muffin tin from oven.

Distribute batter into each cup, filling each a little over half full. Return muffin tin to oven and bake 5 minutes. Reduce heat to 350° and bake about 25 minutes, until golden brown and puffy. Let cool 3 minutes and invert muffin tin. Serve warm.

Entrees

Back to Nature Burger

Buddha's Pot Pie

Cheese Enchiladas Verde

Cheese Polenta

Laurel Canyon Lasagna

Passover Pizza

Pumpkin Pasta

Ratatouille Normandy

Savory Mushroom Tart

Shepherd's Cottage Pie

Back to Nature Burger

Serves 4

2 tablespoons bulgur wheat

½ purple onion

4 cups button mushrooms

½ cup celery

1 teaspoon minced garlic

2 tablespoons olive oil

⅓ cup olives, chopped

½ cup rolled oats

2 tablespoons low-fat cottage cheese

½ cup brown rice, cooked

½ cup mozzarella cheese, shredded

2 tablespoons cheddar cheese, shredded

½ cup hot vegetable broth (I recommend my Very Veggie Broth, see page 71)

Salt and pepper to taste

1 tablespoon cornstarch

¼ cup water

6 tablespoons cornmeal

Mayonnaise

6 to 12 large slices of tomatoes

4 to 6 hamburger buns

This is the meatless, soy-free burger I had been waiting for! It's as satisfying as a Big Mac without the meat, fat, and cholesterol. The cheeses provide protein, and the mushrooms and brown rice give it an earthy flavor. Make as meatballs in spaghetti or stroganoff by just rolling them into ping-pong–size balls instead of patties.

Place bulgur wheat in a small bowl with boiling water. Let soak for 45 minutes. Meanwhile, chop onion, mushrooms, and celery. In a medium skillet, sauté onion, mushrooms, celery, and garlic in olive oil over medium heat for 5 minutes. Set aside.

In a large bowl, combine drained bulgur wheat, olives, oats, sautéed vegetables, cottage cheese, rice, cheeses, and vegetable broth. Mix well. Blend in a blender or food processor in small batches, adding a little water if mixture is too dry. Pour all of the mixture into a bowl. Add salt and pepper. Mix cornstarch in ¼ cup of water. Shape into patties, rolling each patty in cornmeal to keep from sticking. Fry patties in olive oil for 5 minutes on each side over high heat until brown.

Liberally spray a baking sheet covered with aluminum foil with nonstick cooking spray. Remove patties from skillet and place on baking sheet. Bake at 350° for 10 minutes on each side. Garnish burgers with mayonnaise and tomato slices, and place on toasted, warm hamburger buns.

Buddha's Pot Pie

Serves 4

2 ready-made pie crusts, defrosted

1 cup Gardein Chick'n Scaloppini

2 tablespoons olive oil

½ cup shallots, diced

1 cup celery, diced

½ cup carrots, diced

¾ cup frozen peas, thawed

2 medium-sized potatoes, peeled and cubed

¾ cup vegetable broth (I recommend my Very Veggie Broth, see page 71)

1 teaspoon paprika

1 teaspoon garlic powder

2 tablespoons unbleached flour

Buddha's Pot Pie is the ultimate comfort food for autumn or winter. The delicate flavors of Gardein Chick'n Scaloppini cubes combined with carrots and potatoes is the taste of home.

Set aside pie crusts. Defrost "chick'n" and cut into small cubes. Sauté "chick'n" in 1 tablespoon of oil for 3 minutes.

In a large saucepan, heat remaining oil over medium heat. Add shallots, celery, carrots, and peas. Fry for 6 minutes. Add potatoes, broth, paprika, and garlic powder. Stir in flour. Cover, boil, reduce heat, and simmer for 5 minutes. Remove saucepan from stove and stir in "chick'n" and peas.

Preheat oven to 375°. Spoon filling into four 1-cup ramekin dishes until they are full to the top. Cut pie crusts into 4 circles slightly wider than the tops of 4 ramekin dishes. Place pie crust circles on top of each ramekin dish and press. Crimp the edges gently with fork tines. Poke a hole in the center of each pot pie crust. Place ramekins on a cookie sheet in the oven. Bake for 35 to 40 minutes, until golden brown on top.

I made two large tubs of these enchiladas for a church potluck dinner. They were very highly praised and eaten quickly. You can fill them with most anything. Try red bell peppers, mushrooms, or tomatoes. The flavor of old Mexico!

Cheese Enchiladas Verde

Makes 24 enchiladas

2 jars (16 oz. each) salsa verde
24 small corn tortillas
5 cups cheddar cheese, shredded and divided
3 cups green onions, sliced fine and divided
2 cups black olives, sliced
1 cup tomatoes, diced and divided
2 cups white mushrooms, diced fine
1 tablespoon chili powder
Salt and pepper to taste
1 bunch of cilantro, chopped

Spray two 13 x 9 cake pans with nonstick cooking spray. Pour ½ cup of salsa verde into the bottom of each pan. Set aside.

Wrap 3 tortillas at a time in a paper towel and cook tortillas in the microwave oven on half power about 70 seconds. Remove from oven and place on paper towels. Spread each tortilla onto a cutting board. Fill with 1 tablespoon cheese, 1 teaspoon olives, and 1 teaspoon green onion. Add 1 teaspoon each of tomatoes and mushrooms. Add ½ teaspoon of salsa verde. Sprinkle with chili powder, salt, pepper, and cilantro. Roll tortilla up like a thin burrito and place in baking pan seam side down. Continue filling, rolling, and placing each tortilla in pan until you have 12 in each pan.

If you are storing enchiladas for a later serving, cover pan with aluminum foil and place in the refrigerator. Thrity-five minutes before serving, preheat oven to 350°. Remove tortillas from refrigerator. Pour 2 cups of salsa verde over each pan of 12 tortillas. Spread evenly with a dinner knife so that all the enchiladas are coated and moist. Sprinkle with 1½ cups of cheese, tomatoes, chili powder, and cilantro.

Bake 25 to 30 minutes, covered in foil. Uncover and bake for another 5 minutes. Add remaining green onions and serve.

Cheese Polenta

Serves 6 to 10

1 cup cornmeal
1 cup cold water
Pinch salt
3 cups boiling water
1 tablespoon chives, chopped fine
1 tablespoon parsley
½ cup frozen corn, thawed
1 cup crumbled blue cheese
Basil leaves (garnish)
2 tablespoons melted butter

This tasty, simple, and versatile cornmeal loaf is best served warm with a buttery sauce. A perfect potluck dish, it goes well with a green salad.

Combine in a large saucepan cornmeal, cold water, and salt. Stir well and add boiling water. Stir again over a medium flame about 5 minutes. Add chives and parsley and bring mixture to a boil. Stir in the corn and cheese. Reduce heat and let simmer about 25 minutes, stirring frequently until mixture thickens.

Spray a loaf pan generously with nonstick cooking spray. Pour polenta mixture into loaf pan. Cover with foil and refrigerate overnight. Preheat oven to 375°. Invert loaf pan onto a foil baking dish or cookie sheet. Bake polenta for 20 minutes. Garnish with basil leaves, if desired. Warm 2 tablespoons of butter and pour over warmed slices.

Laurel Canyon Lasagna

Serves 8

This is the easiest lasagna recipe I have ever made. The mushrooms, pesto, and olives give it a hearty and satisfying blend with the three cheeses.

2 cups white mushrooms sliced, divided
1 jar (26 oz.) pasta sauce
12 to 14 lasagna noodles, raw
2 tablespoons pesto, divided
1 package (15 oz.) ricotta cheese
2 cups mozzarella cheese, shredded
¼ cup Parmesan cheese, grated
1 cup black olives, sliced
1 teaspoon parsley
1 teaspoon garlic powder
1 teaspoon cilantro
1 tablespoon olive oil

Pour 1 cup of pasta sauce in an 11 x 7–inch baking pan. Top with 6 or 7 lasagna noodles, overlaid horizontally. Cover with half of the pesto. Add ricotta cheese, smooth with a dinner knife like frosting, and 1 cup of mozzarella. Sprinkle half of the Parmesan and add half the mushrooms and olives. Top with 1 cup of pasta sauce and 1 tablespoon pesto. Smooth with dinner knife so all is covered well with sauce. Cover with another layer of lasagna noodles. Top with remaining sauce, mushrooms, olives, the remaining Parmesan, and seasonings.

Preheat oven to 375°. Cover lasagna with foil and bake for 1 hour and 15 minutes. Uncover and top with remaining cup of mozzarella cheese. Drizzle with olive oil. Let stand 10 minutes, cut, and serve.

You don't have to be Jewish to enjoy Passover Pizza anytime. This is the perfect thin-crust pizza! I brought this dish to a Passover Seder and it was eaten up in no time. It can be eaten at any time, but the cheese must be "kosher for Passover" to be eaten during Passover. Choose any toppings you'd like, mushrooms, olives, onions, etc. But remember: Anything too soggy on top of the matzo will make it cave in and it won't stay firm.

Passover Pizza

Serves 2 to 4

1 can (14 oz.) whole peeled tomatoes
2 whole matzo sheets, unbroken
2 cups cheddar or Swiss cheese, kosher
   for Passover, grated and divided
1 cup grated kosher Parmesan cheese
Salt and pepper
2 tablespoons olive oil, divided
Fresh chives and cilantro, chopped fine

Preheat oven to 480°. Drain tomatoes in a strainer, catching the juice for another recipe. Remove all the moisture you can from tomatoes by flattening them on a cutting board with the bottom of a slotted spoon. Shape into round flat pieces.

Place matzos on a foil baking sheet. Carefully spread half of the grated first cheese and sprinkle with salt and pepper. Transfer matzos to oven. Bake for about 5 minutes until bubbly with cheese melted. Remove matzos from oven.

Add dried tomatoes strategically on matzos. Add the other half of the first cheese and return to the oven to bake another 10 minutes. Remove matzos from oven and add half of Parmesan onto each.

Heat oil in a large skillet. With a flat spatula, carefully place matzos one at a time in the skillet and fry the matzo until the bottom is a crisp, golden brown. Plate matzos and drizzle with warm olive oil from skillet. Garnish with herbs.

Pumpkin Pasta

Serves 4

4 tablespoons unsalted butter
¾ cup onion, finely chopped
2 celery stalks, chopped fine
Salt to taste
1 cup pumpkin pulp, seeded
1 teaspoon nutmeg
1 tablespoon dry white wine
6 cups water
1 package (12 oz.) bow-tie pasta
1 cup sour cream
4 tablespoons Parmesan cheese
1 cup reserved pasta water
2 teaspoons parsley flakes
1 teaspoon olive oil

Melt butter over low heat in a saucepan. Add onions, celery, and salt. Sauté for 15 minutes. Add pumpkin, nutmeg, and wine. Cover and simmer over low flame for 20 minutes, stirring frequently.

In a separate pot, boil 6 cups of water over high heat. Add bow-tie pasta and a pinch of salt. Cook pasta al dente, following package instructions. Drain pasta, reserve 1 cup of pasta water, and set aside pasta in a large bowl.

Remove pumpkin sauce from heat. Stir in sour cream, Parmesan cheese, reserved pasta water, and parsley. Mix well and combine with drained pasta in a large bowl. Drizzle with oil and serve.

Ratatouille Normandy

Serves 8

4 large potatoes, peeled and cut into cubes
3 medium eggplants, peeled
4 yellow bell peppers
½ cup olive oil, divided
4 zucchinis, cut in rounds
1 purple onion, chopped
1 yellow onion, chopped
1 teaspoon minced garlic
1 teaspoon French tarragon
1 teaspoon herbes de Provence
1 can (14 oz.) tomatoes
⅓ cup canned tomato juice
2 teaspoons basil leaves, chopped
6 cherry tomatoes
1 tablespoon salt, divided
Pepper to taste

Visiting Normandy, France, the site of D-Day, 1944 in 2012, I had a delicious and hearty version of this French classic. This is a much simpler recipe than is usually found in French cookbooks. There is no need to sauté each vegetable separately. Bump up the protein by adding white beans, if desired. The potatoes are the Normandy touch.

Preheat oven to broil. Place potatoes in salted water. Steam for 15 minutes until soft. Turn off heat and cover pan. Slice eggplants into rounds. Place on a cutting board and sprinkle generously with salt. Let eggplants sweat for 25 minutes. Meanwhile, slice peppers in half and place on a cookie sheet sprayed with nonstick spray. Broil for 10 minutes. Remove peppers from oven and place in a bowl, covered, for 10 minutes. Rinse off eggplants and pat dry with a paper towel.

On a baking sheet, pour 2 tablespoons oil and coat eggplant slices. Add zucchini and toss with 2 tablespoons oil. Reduce oven heat to 400° and bake the eggplants and zucchinis for 15 minutes. Uncover peppers, seed, and cut into julienne strips. Place in a large clear glass bowl.

In a skillet, warm remaining oil. Add onions, minced garlic, tarragon, and herbes de Provence and sauté for 5 minutes. Stir in canned tomatoes and juice. Cook covered for 5 minutes. Remove zucchinis and eggplant from oven and pour into bowl with peppers. Turn off heat and remove onion mixture. Add onion mixture to the bowl. Drain potato cubes and add to the bowl. Toss all ingredients gently. Drizzle with remaining warm olive oil. Garnish with basil, cherry tomatoes, and salt and pepper.

Savory Mushroom Tart

Serves 6 to 8

1 ready-made pie crust

1 tablespoon olive oil

2 tablespoons unsalted butter, divided

3 cups button mushrooms, sliced

1 cup celery, diced

1 cup purple onion, diced

1 teaspoon minced garlic

1 teaspoon chives, diced fine

2 teaspoons parsley flakes

1 teaspoon thyme

2 teaspoons unbleached flour

½ cup cream of mushroom soup (see
    page 59, or use Amy's Organic Cream
    of Mushroom Soup)

1 tablespoon low-fat milk

Basil leaves

⅓ cup grated Parmesan cheese

This is my version of an English Savory Mushroom Tart. This recipe has appeared at Amy's Organic Kitchen website.

Preheat oven to 350°. Prepare pie crust and set aside. In a large skillet, heat olive oil over medium flame. Add butter, mushrooms, celery, onions, and garlic. Sauté for 10 minutes. Remove from heat and use a strainer to transfer mixture to a large bowl. Add spices to bowl and mix well.

Heat butter in a saucepan. Stir in flour. Pour in soup and milk. Mix gradually while stirring. Remove saucepan from heat and stir flour mix into mushroom mix in the bowl. Stir in cheese. Pour bowl mixture into pie crust. Bake for 40 minutes, or until tart is golden brown. Garnish with Parmesan and basil leaves. Slice and serve.

Shepherd's Cottage Pie

Serves 4 to 6

3 potatoes peeled and diced

1⅓ cups water

½ teaspoon salt

2 tablespoons butter

¾ cup low-fat milk

1 tablespoon olive oil

1 tablespoon minced garlic

1 medium onion, chopped

4 celery stalks, chopped

1 can (14 oz.) diced tomatoes, drained

1 cup frozen corn

½ cup dry white wine

½ teaspoon soy sauce

Salt and pepper to taste

1 cup cheddar cheese, shredded

1 teaspoon paprika

This is an Old English traditional favorite pub grub meal with a new vegetarian twist. I've removed the meat and stuffed this crust-less pie with nutritional vegetables and savory spices.

Steam the potatoes for 15 minutes in just enough water to cover them. Add salt, butter, and milk. Using a potato masher, mash and stir potatoes until smooth. Set aside.

In a large saucepan, heat oil and garlic for 1 minute. Add onions and celery. Sauté for 1 minute. Stir in tomatoes and corn. Simmer for 5 minutes, covered. Add wine and soy sauce. Bring to a boil. Reduce heat, cooking for 5 minutes more.

Spray a baking dish or pie tin liberally with nonstick cooking spray. Transfer vegetable mixture to pie tin. Cover with mashed potatoes carefully, as if you were frosting a cake. Sprinkle with cheese and paprika. Bake at 375° for 35 to 40 minutes, until golden brown.

Desserts

American Apple Pie

California Cheesecake

Chocolate Dream Cake

Country Pumpkin Pie

Creamy Carrot Cake

Crème Brûlée

Key Lime Pie

Scotch Blondies

Shoo-Fly Pecan Pie

Snowball Cookies

American Apple Pie

Serves 8

2 deep dish pie shells
6 to 7 apples (Pink Lady, Fuji, Granny
   Smith)
¾ cup sugar, divided
½ teaspoon allspice
½ teaspoon cinnamon, divided
½ teaspoon ground ginger
2½ tablespoons cornstarch
Dash of salt
3 tablespoons lemon juice
2 tablespoons unsalted butter, cut into
   small squares

This classic American dessert is perfect for any picnic or dinner. Why not serve it up for Memorial Day, Fourth of July, President's Day, Flag Day, or even Thanksgiving? Add ice cream or whipped cream and you have a mouth-watering flavor riot on your hands. I used a blend of the three apples, but use any apples you'd like. Kids love this!

Preheat oven to 400°. Set aside two pie shells. Peel, core, and slice apples into small ¼-inch pieces. Place apple pieces in a large bowl. Set aside. In another bowl, mix sugar, spices, cornstarch, and salt. Add apples and combine well. Squeeze lemon juice over apple mix.

Spoon apple mix carefully into one of the pie shells. Place butter pieces carefully over pie filling. Apply second pie shell on top of pie filling. Press edges to seal completely. Cut excess edges with scissors to trim the rim. Flute edges with the tines of a fork to further seal. Brush the top of the pie crust with water. Sprinkle 1 tablespoon sugar mixed with cinnamon on top. Cut 5 slits on top of pie with a knife.

Place pie on a baking sheet in the oven and bake for 15 minutes. Reduce heat to 350° and bake 45 minutes, until crust is golden brown. Let cool and serve.

California Cheesecake

Serves 8 to 10

CRUST

1¾ cups graham cracker crumbs

3 tablespoons sugar

3 tablespoons unsalted butter, melted

FILLING

3 blocks (8 oz. each) softened light cream
   cheese

¾ cup sugar

2 tablespoons lemon juice

1 teaspoon vanilla extract

1 teaspoon nutmeg

3 eggs

TOPPING

1½ cups reduced fat sour cream

3 tablespoons sugar

1 teaspoon vanilla extract

1 teaspoon lemon juice

New York cheesecake is a delicious dessert tradition, for sure. But California, the Left Coast, will not be outdone! This plain, pure, and classic cheesecake proves it. It's light and luscious, with just the right blend of sweet, creamy, and lemony flavors. Perfection!

Preheat oven to 325°. Spray a glass 9-inch pie pan with nonstick cooking spray. Crumble graham crackers until they resemble breadcrumbs. Add sugar and butter. Combine well. Using a spoon, press graham mixture into the bottom of the pie pan. Bake crust 10 minutes. Remove from oven and set aside.

In a large bowl, using a hand mixer, beat cream cheese, sugar, lemon juice, vanilla, and nutmeg about 2 minutes on medium speed. Add eggs one at a time, continuing to beat on low after each egg until filling is smooth and well combined. Pour filling over crust and bake for 1 hour.

In a small bowl, combine sour cream, sugar, vanilla, and lemon juice well. Stir until smooth. Remove cheesecake from oven and cool for 15 minutes. Spread topping carefully on cheesecake with a dinner knife. Bake for 10 minutes. Refrigerate, covered, at least 3 hours or overnight. Slice and serve.

Chocolate Dream Cake

Serves 8 to 10

Egg-less, light, chocolate, and luscious, this healthy, diet-conscious dessert is perfect for birthdays, holidays, and special occasions!

CAKE

3 cups unbleached flour

1 cup granulated sugar

1 cup light brown sugar

6 tablespoons unsweetened cocoa powder

1½ teaspoons baking soda

¼ teaspoon salt

½ cup cooking oil

1 tablespoon lemon juice

1 tablespoon mineral water

2 cups cold water

2 teaspoons vanilla extract

FROSTING

1 stick unsalted butter

1 1-pound box confectioners (powdered) sugar

½ cup unsweetened cocoa powder

⅓ cup low-fat milk

2 teaspoons vanilla extract

CAKE

Preheat oven to 350°. Spray two 8-inch round cake pans with cooking spray and set aside. Combine flour, sugars, cocoa powder, baking soda, and salt in a large bowl. Add oil, lemon juice, mineral water, cold water, and vanilla extract. Beat with a mixer for 2 minutes until smooth.

Fill each pan ¾ full. Set pans on top rack of the oven. Bake for 30 minutes until toothpick test comes out clean. Remove pans from oven. Gently dig a dinner knife around the circumference of each cake pan to loosen cakes. Invert cake pan #1 and place on a cake plate. Invert cake pan #2 and place on another plate. Let cake layers cool while you prepare frosting.

FROSTING

In a medium-sized bowl, beat butter, sugar, and cocoa powder with a mixer for 3 minutes. Gradually add milk and vanilla. Beat until smooth. If frosting is too thick, add more milk; if too thin, add more cocoa powder. Refrigerate for 1 hour or overnight, if you have the time.

After cake layers have cooled, frost the bottom cake layer completely. Place top layer carefully on top of the bottom layer. Frost thoroughly with a dinner knife. Continue frosting the top layer, in between portions, and any spots you may have missed. Cut cake and serve.

Country Pumpkin Pie

Serves 6 to 8

1 can (15 oz.) pumpkin puree

1 teaspoon vanilla

1 teaspoon cinnamon

1 teaspoon nutmeg

1 teaspoon ground ginger

1 teaspoon allspice

Dash of salt

1 can (14 oz.) sweetened condensed milk

1 egg slightly beaten

1 deep-dish pie shell (9-inch)

2 cups whipped cream

6 Autumn Leaves icing decorations
   (optional)

So easy! This traditional, old-fashioned holiday favorite has a new twist and a zestier flavor. The ginger and allspice do the trick, and because you are using sweetened condensed milk, there's no need to measure sugar and no chance of the pie being too sweet. Serve anytime, but especially on Halloween, Thanksgiving, or Christmas.

Combine pumpkin puree, vanilla, and spices in a large mixing bowl. Stir in condensed milk and egg until completely blended. Pour into deep-dish pie shell. Cover pie crust rim with aluminum foil to avoid burning.

Bake at 450° for 15 minutes. Reduce heat to 350° and bake 35 to 40 minutes. Remove pie from oven and let cool. Add icing decorations. Slice pie, add a dollop of whipped cream on each piece, and serve.

Creamy Carrot Cake

Serves 4 to 6

CAKE

1 cup sifted unbleached flour

½ cup brown sugar

½ teaspoon baking powder

Pinch of salt

½ teaspoon ground cinnamon

½ teaspoon allspice

1 teaspoon vanilla extract

¼ cup vegetable oil

1 egg beaten

1½ cups carrots, boiled and pureed

½ cup slivered almonds

1 cup unsweetened shredded coconut

FROSTING:

1 block (8 oz.) low-fat cream cheese
   (room temperature)

1 cup sifted powdered sugar

1 tablespoon lemon juice

I have had my share of carrot cakes that taste like a liquified brick. Heavy, too sweet, dull, and indigestible. My one-layer version will not disappoint. The sugar level is low and the low-fat cream cheese frosting will cut the heavy calories. You could use unsweetened pureed baby food carrots to save time.

Preheat oven to 350°. Spray nonstick cooking spray on an 8-inch cake pan. In a large bowl, combine first six dry ingredients. Stir in vanilla, oil, and egg. Add pureed carrots and beat well with an electric mixer or a hand blender. Fold in almonds and coconut. Pour mixture into prepared pan. Bake for 45 minutes. Check cake with a toothpick. When toothpick comes out clean, it is done. Set aside.

For the frosting, mash softened cream cheese well. Add powdered sugar and lemon juice. Beat with a hand blender until smooth. Refrigerate for at least 1 hour.

Invert cooled cake onto cake serving plate. Frost cake carefully with a dinner knife. Garnish with carrot slices, if desired.

No blowtorch required! This tasty and creamy French classic couldn't be simpler. Impress your dinner guests with this beautiful and simple dessert. Top with a dollop of whipped cream, if desired.

Crème Brûlée

Serves 4

3 egg yolks
⅓ cup white sugar
1 teaspoon vanilla extract
1 cup heavy cream
3 tablespoons brown sugar
Whipped cream (optional)

Preheat oven to 300°. In a large bowl, whisk together egg yolks, sugar, and vanilla. In a saucepan, bring the heavy cream just to a simmer over low heat. Add the egg yolk mixture to the heavy cream, stirring to combine.

Form a double boiler by bringing 2 inches of water to a simmer in an oven-safe pan over low heat. Place the cream mixture bowl over the oven-safe pan. Place double boiler into heated oven and bake for 25 minutes. Test with a toothpick to be sure that mixture has set. Remove cream mixture from oven. Scoop cream into 4 oven-proof ramekins or dessert cups. Chill in refrigerator for 1 to 2 hours.

Heat oven to broil. Sprinkle brown sugar evenly over the cream mixture in the ramekins. Place ramekins directly under broiler for 2 minutes. After the sugar has browned, return desserts to refrigerator to chill 15 minutes, or up to 1 hour. Spoon a dollop of whipped cream over each ramekin. Voilà!

Key Lime Pie

Serves 8

5 egg yolks, beaten
1 can (14 oz.) sweetened condensed milk
½ cup lime juice
1 teaspoon green sugar
1 9-inch pie crust
1 lime, sliced into thin rounds (garnish)

So refreshing, easy, and cool! A great summertime pie, or anytime pie. Key Lime Pie is an American classic from Florida. With just a few ingredients, it is easy to whip up when those unexpected relatives drop by.

Preheat oven to 375°. With a hand mixer, blend egg yolks, milk, lime juice, and sugar. Pour into unbaked pie crust. Bake for 15 minutes. Cool in refrigerator for 30 minutes to 24 hours. Garnish with lime slices.

Scotch Blondies

Serves 12

BLONDIES

1 cup unbleached flour
½ teaspoon baking powder
¼ teaspoon baking soda
1 stick (½ cup) and 1 tablespoon unsalted
   butter
½ cup brown sugar
1½ tablespoons ground coffee
Dash of salt
1 egg
1 teaspoon vanilla extract
1 teaspoon scotch whiskey

TOPPING

1 tablespoon melted unsalted butter
2 tablespoons scotch whiskey
1 teaspoon vanilla extract
¾ cup powdered sugar
1 cup unsalted sliced almonds

A classic coffee bar favorite, in the U.K., blondies have been around for years. This delicious variation includes scotch whiskey in the batter and the topping. Everyone loves brownies, but the subtle caramel-like taste of blondies cannot be beat!

Preheat oven to 350°. Spray a 9 x 12-inch square baking pan with nonstick cooking spray. In a large bowl, whisk flour, baking powder, and baking soda together. Melt stick of butter and pour into the dry mixture. Stir in brown sugar, coffee, and salt. Stir in egg, vanilla, and whiskey. Combine well. Pour mixture into prepared pan. Bake for 25 minutes. Remove pan from oven and cool for 30 minutes.

To make topping, whisk butter, whiskey, and vanilla together. Add powdered sugar gradually, stir until thick. Spread topping across cooled Blondies. Using a fork or chopstick, draw diagonal crisscross lines across the cooled Blondies. Sprinkle with slivered almonds. Allow topping 1 hour to dry. Using a very sharp, wet knife, cut Blondies into 12 squares, wetting knife after each cut. Serve at room temperature.

Shoo-Fly Pecan Pie

Serves 6 to 8

FILLING

1 deep-dish pie shell

½ cup light corn syrup

¼ cup dark brown sugar

1 egg, beaten

½ teaspoon baking soda

½ cup hot water

TOPPING

1 cup unbleached flour

3 tablespoons shortening

⅔ cup dark brown sugar

1 teaspoon each of allspice, nutmeg, cinnamon

Dash of salt

½ cup pecan pieces

Shoo-Fly pie originated with the Pennsylvania Dutch and was also popular in Southern cooking. The original pie was made with molasses. The name "Shoo-Fly Pie" first appeared in print in 1926, and probably got its name because the molasses attracted flies that had to be shooed away. My version uses light corn syrup and is topped with yummy pecan pieces.

Preheat oven to 350°. Set aside pie shell. For the filling, in a large bowl, combine corn syrup, sugar, and egg. Stir well. In a small cup, pour baking soda into hot water. Stir into filling mixture. Pour filling into pie shell. Set aside.

Prepare topping by combining flour, shortening, sugar, spices, and salt in a large bowl. Press and stir with a fork until topping crumbles. Sprinkle the streusel-like crumbs over filling. Top with pecan pieces attractively arranged. Bake for 1 hour. Serve alone or top with plain yogurt, whipped cream, or vanilla ice cream.

Snowball Cookies

Makes 36 cookies

1 cup unsalted butter, softened

2 cups unbleached flour, sifted

1 cup powdered sugar, sifted

A pinch of salt

2 tablespoons unsweetened cocoa powder

¼ cup milk

1 cup flour for dusting

1 teaspoon vanilla extract

1 cup powdered sugar for dusting

1 cup shredded coconut

If you're looking for the perfect White Christmas cookie, this is it. Bake a big batch and box them up for Christmas goody gifts, or serve on Christmas Eve when friends come to call. Be sure to flour your hands well and repeatedly or else this can get messy.

Preheat oven to 400°. In a large bowl, beat butter, sugar, cocoa, milk, and vanilla with a hand mixer until smooth, about 5 minutes. Add flour in batches, gradually beating until well mixed. Add salt.

Prepare cookie sheets with a generous coating of nonstick cooking spray. Cover hands with flour while shaping dough into 1-inch snowballs. Carefully place balls on cookie sheets. Do not crowd because snowballs will expand. Place cookies in oven and bake for 10 minutes. Remove cookie sheets from oven and cool for 10 minutes.

Roll each snowball in powdered sugar. Re-roll each snowball in coconut until they are thoroughly covered. Shake off the excess. Serve on a cookie plate.

Vegetarian Holiday Menu Ideas

New Year's Day Brunch
Waldorf Astoria Salad
Mushroom & Swiss Crepes
Buddha's Pot Pie

Easter Sunday Brunch
Quiche Deluxe
Chickpea Noodle Soup
Le Cobb Salad
Zucchini Pancakes

Cinco de Mayo May 5th Meal
Guacamole & Chips
Gazpacho Gustavo!
Cheese Enchiladas Verde
Shoo-Fly Pecan Pie

Fourth of July Luncheon BBQ
Caesar Salad
Back to Nature Burger
Roquefort Potatoes au Gratin
American Apple Pie

Thanksgiving Dinner
Cranberry Collage Salad
Celery Cream Soup
Pumpkin Pasta
Yorkshire Pudding Puffs
Country Pumpkin Pie

Christmas Eve Dinner
Swiss Cheese Fondue with bread cubes
"We Got the Beet" Salad
Shepherd's Cottage Pie
Snowball Cookies

New Year's Eve Party
Vegetarian Gyozas
Hippie Hummus
Crudité with dip
Caesar Salad
Laurel Canyon Lasagna
Scotch Blondies

Index

Index

About the Author

Sonya Maria Sargent is a self-taught chef. Her recipes have appeared on VegetarianTimes.com, TasteofHome.com, BetterRecipes.com, and AllRecipes.com, among other websites and magazines. Her Savory Mushroom Tart recipe appeared on the Amy's Organic Kitchen website, and her Passover Pizza recipe can be found under Festival Recipes on the Jewish Vegetarian Society U.K. website.

She took third place honors in the 2010 *Vegetarian Times* magazine Reader Holiday Recipes Contest for her Danish Almond Streusel Cake recipe, which was described as "simple and delicious." Also featured in *Vegetarian Times* magazine was her Asian Autumn Salad recipe. It was chosen number two in that issue's "Fab 5" Recipes.

Sonya is also an accomplished musician, singer, composer, performer, recording artist, and guitarist. Her CD recordings of her original music releases, titled, "Seven," "Blue Eyes," "Sonya," "Sonoma," "Christmas Doll," "Sonya Live!," and her latest, "Follow Your Dreams," can be purchased through cdbaby.com.

She has resided with her husband, Ken Sargent, in L.A.'s Laurel Canyon neighborhood for more than twenty-five years. During that time, she has been creating innovative recipes for her family, neighbors, and friends. She was inspired to write *The Laurel Canyon Vegetarian Cookbook* after seeing the 2009 film *Julie and Julia*, starring Meryl Streep and Amy Adams. At present, she is studying French cooking.